**When Paul became a Christian he preached in Damascus.**

The new Christians shared everything together.

**Dorcas loved to help everyone around her.**

**While Peter slept God sent him a strange dream.**

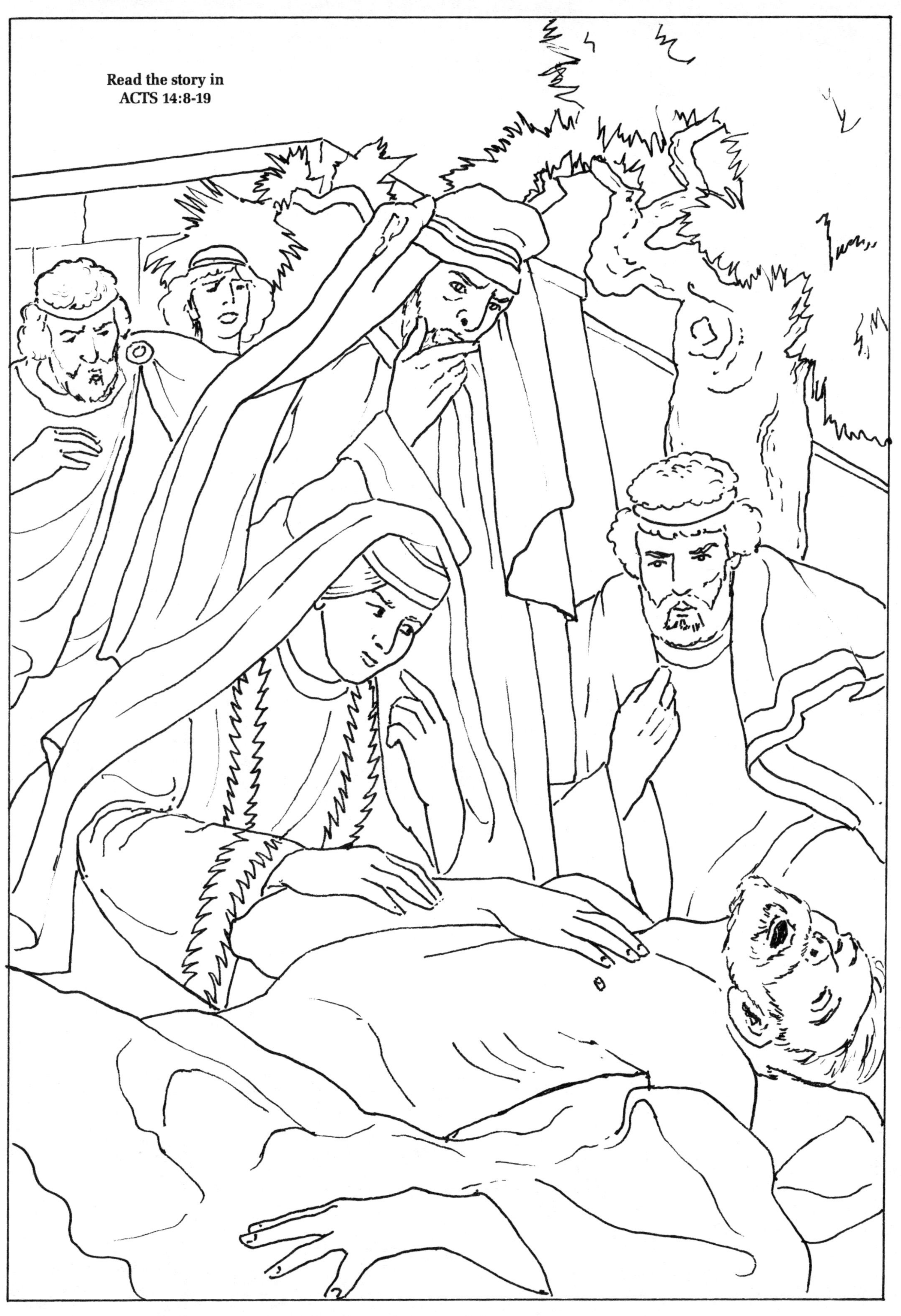


**The people thought that Paul was dead.**

Paul, Barnabas and Mark go on a journey.

**Paul meets Timothy's family.**

**'Come to Macedonia,' said the man in Paul's vision.**

**The women learned about Jesus from Timothy and Paul.**

Adventure in a Philippian gaol.

**Apollos learns from Priscilla and Aquila.**

**Bonfire at Ephesus.**

**Paul talks about Jesus to Felix and Drusilla.**

King Agrippa listens to Paul.

They all swam to safety as the ship broke up.

**Paul, a prisoner in his own home.**